MY SiDEWALKS ON
SCOTT FORESMAN
READING STREET

Assessment Book

Level
E

PEARSON
Scott Foresman

Editorial Offices: Glenview, Illinois • Parsippany, New Jersey
New York, New York
Sales Offices: Boston, Massachusetts • Duluth, Georgia
Glenview, Illinois • Coppell, Texas • Sacramento, California • Mesa, Arizona

0-328-21396-9

3 4 5 6 7 8 9 10 V031 15 14 13 12 11 10 09 08 07 06

Table of Contents

My Sidewalks, Level E Intensive Reading Intervention Assessment Plan

4-Step Plan for Assessment

1 Diagnosis and Placement
2 Monitor Progress
3 Evaluate Student Progress
4 Exiting the Program

The assessments in this handbook will enable you to gather valuable information about your students' understanding and mastery of reading skills before, during, and after instruction.

Step 1 Diagnosis and Placement

Use the Placement Test with individual at-risk students who have been identified through baseline test performance, work in the core reading program, and observation. Administer the *My Sidewalks* Placement Test to determine the level at which to begin students in *My Sidewalks* and to identify the areas of literacy (word reading, fluency, or comprehension) that are problematic for each student.

Placement Test Overview

This Placement Test is designed to help you identify the appropriate level at which to begin students who will use the *My Sidewalks Intensive Reading Intervention* program.

The Placement Test for Level E (pp. 16–19) has four parts. These subtests are to be administered with individual at-risk students who have been identified through baseline test performance, work in the core reading program, and observation.

The chart below shows the number of items in each subtest. Estimated times are given for planning purposes only. Allow as much time as needed for each student to complete the screening. You may administer this screening in two or three sittings.

Subtest	Number of Items	Estimated Time
1 Word Reading: Phonics	20	1 minute
2 Word Reading: High-Frequency Words	20	1 minute
3 Fluency and Comprehension	WCPM Retelling	12 minutes
4 Word Reading: Benchmark Words	20	1 minute
Total	60	15 minutes

Directions for Administering the Test

Particular directions for each subtest appear on pp. 16–17. The directions in **bold** type are to be read aloud.

Make two copies of the student's test, pp. 18–19, one for the student and one for you to mark. Also make a copy of the Evaluation Chart, p. 15, for each student. Have Benchmark Reader D6 on hand.

Begin with Subtests 1–2. If the student scores less than 80% on Subtests 1–2, discontinue testing. This student may be more appropriately placed in Level D of *My Sidewalks*. If the student scores 80% or better on Subtests 1–2, have the student complete Subtest 3.

Scoring

Record each student's scores on a copy of the Evaluation Chart.

Interpreting the Scores

- If the student scores less than 80% on Subtests 1–2, he or she may be more appropriately placed in Level D of *My Sidewalks* or may require further testing.
- Students who score 80% or better on Subtests 1–2 and who can read the Subtest 3 passage accurately are appropriately placed in Level E of *My Sidewalks*.
- Students who score above 90% on Subtests 1–2 and who read and retell the Subtest 3 passage accurately should continue with Subtest 4. Students who score 80% or better on Subtest 4 should be asked to read Benchmark Reader D6. Students who read Benchmark Reader D6 with 90% accuracy, at a rate of approximately 100 wcpm, and who have a summative retelling score of 3 may be capable of working in a core fifth-grade reading program with instructional emphasis in the areas of need and with strategic intervention.

14   Placement Test Overview

Step 2 Monitor Progress

Use the ongoing assessments found on Day 5 each week in the Teacher's Guides to identify individual instructional needs and to provide appropriate support. Use retellings and the Fluency Progress Chart found in the Teacher's Guides to track each student's progress.

The
Baseball
Reporter

By Ted Fashum
Illustrated by Stacey Schuett

Level E1 Benchmark Reader

Step 3 Evaluate Student Progress

Administer the Unit Tests to check mastery of unit skills. To make instructional decisions at the end of a unit, use end-of-unit assessment results, which include students' performance on Day 5 assessments for that unit, on the Unit Test, and on reading of the unit Benchmark Reader. (Use of the Benchmark Reader is optional.) Use the Record Chart on p. 12 to gather complete end-of-unit information.

Step 4 Exiting the Program

There are two opportunities for students to exit the program—at midyear and at the end of the year. To exit the program, a student must show progress toward grade-level goals. Use the Midyear and End-of-Year Exit Criteria on p. 13 as your guide.

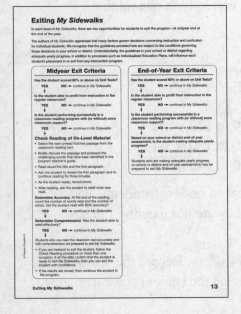

Monitoring Fluency

Ongoing assessment of reading fluency is one of the most valuable measures we have of students' reading skills. One of the most effective ways to assess fluency is taking timed samples of students' oral reading and measuring the number of words correct per minute (wcpm).

How to Assess Fluency

Make one copy of the fluency passage for yourself and one for the student to read. Fluency passages are provided for use in the Unit Tests. Say to the student: **As you read this aloud, I want you to do your best reading and to read as quickly as you can. That doesn't mean it's a race. Just do your best, fast reading. When I say** *begin,* **start reading.**

As the student reads, follow along in your copy. Mark words that are read incorrectly. Explanations of these miscues are found in the Teacher's Guides, Volumes 1 and 2, on page 184.

Incorrect
- omissions
- substitutions
- mispronunciations
- insertions

Correct
- self-corrections within 3 seconds
- repeated words

At the end of one minute, draw a line after the last word that was read. Have the student finish reading, but don't count any words beyond one minute. Arrive at the words correct per minute—wcpm—by counting the total number of words that the student read correctly in one minute.

Fluency Goals

Level E End-of-Year Goal = 120–140 wcpm

Target Goals by Unit

Unit 1 70 to 90 wcpm	**Unit 4** 100 to 120 wcpm
Unit 2 80 to 100 wcpm	**Unit 5** 110 to 130 wcpm
Unit 3 90 to 110 wcpm	**Unit 6** 120 to 140 wcpm

Note: The fluency goals at the high end of the range are more typical of on-level students, and students in intensive intervention may be progressing well even if they are not meeting fluency benchmarks.

Fluency Progress Chart Copy the chart on the next page for each student. Record the score for each timed reading by coloring in the column up to that point or having the student color it.

Student's Name _____

Fluency Progress Chart

Individual Progress Notes

Unit 1	
Unit 2	
Unit 3	
Unit 4	
Unit 5	
Unit 6	

Level E Fluency Progress Chart

	Unit 1	Unit 2	Unit 3	Unit 4	Unit 5	Unit 6
150						
145						
140						
135						
130						
125						
120						
115						
110						
105						
100						
95						
90						
85						
80						
75						
70						
65						
60						
55						
50						
45						

Scoring Rubrics for Retelling

If students have difficulty retelling, then use the prompts for expository or narrative retelling below to help move them toward fluent retelling.

Expository Prompts
- What was this selection mostly about?
- What is it important to know about _____?
- What did you learn about _____?

Scoring Rubric Expository Retelling			
Score	**3**	**2**	**1**
Topic	Identifies the main topic with some details	Identifies the main topic with no details	Does not identify the main topic
Important Ideas	Identifies main ideas	Gives limited information about main ideas	Does not identify any main ideas or gives inaccurate information about ideas
Conclusions	Draws defensible conclusions about the text	Draws conclusions about the text with limited support	Draws inaccurate or no conclusions about the text

Note No score indicates no response.

Narrative Prompts
- Who is this story about? Tell me more about _____.
- Where or when does the story take place?
- What is the problem or goal? How is the problem solved or the goal reached?

Scoring Rubric Narrative Retelling			
Score	**3**	**2**	**1**
Characters	Identifies the main characters and adds details about each	Identifies the main characters without providing details	Is unable to distinguish the main characters
Setting	Identifies the time and location	Omits details of time or location	Does not identify time or location
Plot	Accurately describes the beginning, middle, and end of the story	Retells parts of the story with gaps that affect meaning	Retelling has no sense of story

Note No score indicates no response.

Using the Retelling Charts
- Use a copy of the Expository or Narrative Retelling Chart, pp. 9–10, to record the student's retelling scores for each unit.
- Circle the student's rubric scores for the Retelling Criteria.
- Circle the student's Unit Summative Score. Use the Summative Score Guidelines at the top of pp. 9–10.
- Record the Summative Score on the student's Record Sheet for Unit Tests.

Summative Score Guidelines		
3 Rubric Score of all 3s in all Retelling Criteria	**2** Rubric Score of 3s, 2s, and some 1s in all Retelling Criteria	**1** Rubric Score of 1s or no response in all Retelling Criteria

Summative Scores (Circle one.)	Unit 1 Expository 3 2 1	Unit 2 Expository 3 2 1	Unit 3 Expository 3 2 1

Expository Retelling Chart

Retelling Criteria	Teacher-Aided Response	Student-Generated Response	Rubric Score
Topic			3 2 1
Important Ideas			3 2 1
Conclusions			3 2 1

Note No score indicates no response.

Narrative Retelling Chart

Retelling Criteria	Teacher-Aided Response	Student-Generated Response	Rubric Score
Characters			3 2 1
Setting			3 2 1
Plot			3 2 1

Note No score indicates no response.

© Pearson Education E

Retelling Charts

Student's Name _____ Level E

Summative Scores (Circle one.)	Unit 4 Narrative 3 2 1	Unit 5 Narrative 3 2 1	Unit 6 Narrative 3 2 1

Expository Retelling Chart

Retelling Criteria	Teacher-Aided Response	Student-Generated Response	Rubric Score
Topic			3 2 1
Important Ideas			3 2 1
Conclusions			3 2 1

Note No score indicates no response.

Narrative Retelling Chart

Retelling Criteria	Teacher-Aided Response	Student-Generated Response	Rubric Score
Characters			3 2 1
Setting			3 2 1
Plot			3 2 1

Note No score indicates no response.

© Pearson Education E

My Sidewalks, Level E Intensive Reading Intervention

Using Benchmark Readers

There is one Benchmark Reader for each unit in *My Sidewalks*. The Benchmark Readers can serve as alternative tools for assessment. Benchmark Readers may be used

- to help determine a student's appropriate placement in *My Sidewalks*
- to measure a student's fluency (WCPM) and comprehension (retelling)
- to assess a student's mastery of phonics skills and high-frequency words for a completed unit, using connected text
- to confirm readiness for starting a new unit

Each Benchmark Reader utilizes the target phonics skills for the unit. Examples of the phonics skills are listed on the inside back cover of the book, along with a word count for measuring words correct per minute. Suggested retelling prompts and the Scoring Rubrics for Retelling on page 8 can be used to assess a student's comprehension of the text.

Level E1 Benchmark Reader

Level E2 Benchmark Reader

Level E3 Benchmark Reader

Level E4 Benchmark Reader

Level E5 Benchmark Reader

Level E6 Benchmark Reader

Record Chart for Unit Tests

		Score Individual/Group		Reteach ✔	Individual Retest Score	Comments
Unit 1	Word Reading: Phonics	/30	/10		/30	
	Concept Vocabulary	/25	/5		/25	
	Fluency WCPM					
	Retelling Score					
Unit 2	Word Reading: Phonics	/30	/10		/30	
	Concept Vocabulary	/25	/5		/25	
	Fluency WCPM					
	Retelling Score					
Unit 3	Word Reading: Phonics	/30	/10		/30	
	Concept Vocabulary	/25	/5		/25	
	Fluency WCPM					
	Retelling Score					
Unit 4	Word Reading: Phonics	/30	/10		/30	
	Concept Vocabulary	/25	/5		/25	
	Fluency WCPM					
	Retelling Score					
Unit 5	Word Reading: Phonics	/30	/10		/30	
	Concept Vocabulary	/25	/5		/25	
	Fluency WCPM					
	Retelling Score					
Unit 6	Word Reading: Phonics	/30	/10		/30	
	Concept Vocabulary	/25	/5		/25	
	Fluency WCPM					
	Retelling Score					

Record Scores Use this chart to record scores for the Level E Unit Tests.

Reteach Reteach phonics skills or provide additional practice with concept words if the student scores below 80% on either portion of the Unit Test.

Retest The Individual Unit Test may be used to retest skills that have been retaught.

To move into the next unit of *My Sidewalks*, students should	The student may be more appropriately placed in *My Sidewalks* Level D if
• score 80% or better on the Unit Test • be able to read and retell the end-of-unit Benchmark Reader accurately • be capable of working in the Level E group based on teacher judgment	• the student makes little progress in Unit 1, scoring 60% or lower on the Unit 1 Test • and is struggling to keep up with the Level E group • and, based on teacher judgment, the Level E materials are not at the student's level

Exiting *My Sidewalks*

In each level of *My Sidewalks*, there are two opportunities for students to exit the program—at midyear and at the end of the year.

The authors of *My Sidewalks* appreciate that many factors govern decisions concerning instruction and curriculum for individual students. We recognize that the guidelines provided here are subject to the conditions governing those decisions in your school or district. Understandably, the guidelines in your school or district regarding adequate yearly progress, in addition to processes such as Individualized Education Plans, will influence each student's placement in or exit from any intervention program.

Midyear Exit Criteria

Has the student scored 80% or above on Unit Tests?

YES ↓   **NO** → continue in *My Sidewalks*

Is the student able to profit from instruction in the regular classroom?

YES ↓   **NO** → continue in *My Sidewalks*

Is the student performing successfully in a classroom reading program with (or without) extra classroom support?

YES ↓   **NO** → continue in *My Sidewalks*

Check Reading of On-Level Material

- Select the next unread fictional passage from the classroom reading text.
- Briefly discuss the passage and preteach the challenging words that have been identified in the program teacher's guide.
- Read aloud the title and the first paragraph.
- Ask the student to reread the first paragraph and to continue reading for three minutes.
- As the student reads, record errors.
- After reading, ask the student to retell what was read.

Determine Accuracy At the end of the reading, count the number of words read and the number of errors. Did the student read with 85% accuracy?

YES ↓   **NO** → continue in *My Sidewalks*

Determine Comprehension Was the student able to retell effectively?

YES ↓   **NO** → continue in *My Sidewalks*

Students who can read the classroom text accurately and with comprehension are prepared to exit *My Sidewalks*.

- If you are hesitant to exit the student, follow the Check Reading procedure on more than one occasion. If all the data confirm that the student is ready to exit *My Sidewalks*, then you can exit the student with confidence.
- If the results are mixed, then continue the student in the program.

End-of-Year Exit Criteria

Has the student scored 80% or above on Unit Tests?

YES ↓   **NO** → continue in *My Sidewalks*

Is the student able to profit from instruction in the regular classroom?

YES ↓   **NO** → continue in *My Sidewalks*

Is the student performing successfully in a classroom reading program with (or without) extra classroom support?

YES ↓   **NO** → continue in *My Sidewalks*

Based on your school or district end-of-year assessment, is the student making adequate yearly progress?

YES ↓   **NO** → continue in *My Sidewalks*

Students who are making adequate yearly progress on school or district end-of-year assessments may be prepared to exit *My Sidewalks*.

Placement Test Overview

This Placement Test is designed to help you identify the appropriate level at which to begin students who will use the *My Sidewalks Intensive Reading Intervention* program.

The Placement Test for Level E (pp. 16–19) has four parts. These subtests are to be administered with individual at-risk students who have been identified through baseline test performance, work in the core reading program, and observation.

The chart below shows the number of items in each subtest. Estimated times are given for planning purposes only. Allow as much time as needed for each student to complete the screening. You may administer this screening in two or three sittings.

Subtest	Number of Items	Estimated Time
1 Word Reading: Phonics	20	1 minute
2 Word Reading: High-Frequency Words	20	1 minute
3 Fluency and Comprehension	WCPM Retelling	12 minutes
4 Word Reading: Benchmark Words	20	1 minute
Total	**60**	**15 minutes**

Directions for Administering the Test

Particular directions for each subtest appear on pp. 16–17. The directions in **bold** type are to be read aloud.

Make two copies of the student's test, pp. 18–19, one for the student and one for you to mark. Also make a copy of the Evaluation Chart, p. 15, for each student. Have Benchmark Reader D6 on hand.

Begin with Subtests 1–2. If the student scores less than 80% on Subtests 1–2, discontinue testing. This student may be more appropriately placed in Level D of *My Sidewalks*. If the student scores 80% or better on Subtests 1–2, have the student complete Subtest 3.

Scoring

Record each student's scores on a copy of the Evaluation Chart.

Interpreting the Scores

- If the student scores less than 80% on Subtests 1–2, he or she may be more appropriately placed in Level D of *My Sidewalks* or may require further testing.
- Students who score 80% or better on Subtests 1–2 and who can read the Subtest 3 passage accurately are appropriately placed in Level E of *My Sidewalks*.
- Students who score above 90% on Subtests 1–2 and who read and retell the Subtest 3 passage accurately should continue with Subtest 4. Students who score 80% or better on Subtest 4 should be asked to read Benchmark Reader D6. Students who read Benchmark Reader D6 with 90% accuracy, at a rate of approximately 100 WCPM, and who have a summative retelling score of 3 may be capable of working in a core fifth-grade reading program with instructional emphasis in the areas of need and with strategic intervention.

Evaluation Chart

1 Word Reading: Phonics

SCORE SUBTEST 1	_____ / 20

2 Word Reading: High-Frequency Words

SCORE SUBTEST 2	_____ / 20

3a Fluency

	_____ WCPM

3b Comprehension: Expository Retelling

Retelling Criteria	Rubric Score		
Topic	3	2	1
Important Ideas	3	2	1
Conclusions	3	2	1
SUMMATIVE SCORE	_____ / 3		

4 Word Reading: Benchmark Words

SCORE SUBTEST 4	_____ / 20

SCORE TOTALS

1 Word Reading: Phonics	_____ / 20
2 Word Reading: High-Frequency Words	_____ / 20
TOTAL SCORE	_____ / 40

Note: Subtest 4 is not part of the Placement Test for most students.

4 Word Reading: Benchmark Words	_____ / 20

PERCENTAGES

	Total Score: Subtests 1–2	Subtest 4
100%	40	20
90%	36	18
80%	32	16

Placement Test

1 Word Reading: Phonics

Display student test page 18. Say

- **Read the words in part 1 aloud. Begin next to the number 1, and read across the line. Read all four lines. Stop when you get to the end of part 1.**

Mark correct responses on your copy of the test page. Record the number correct on the Evaluation Chart.

2 Word Reading: High-Frequency Words

Display student test page 18. Say

- **Read the words in part 2 aloud. Begin next to the number 2, and read across the line. Read all four lines. Stop when you get to the end of part 2.**

Mark correct responses on your copy of the test page. Record the number correct on the Evaluation Chart.

3 Fluency and Comprehension

Assess Fluency Display student test page 19.

- **Now I will ask you to read a selection aloud to me.**
- **Use your best reading as you read this selection titled "Instant Information."**

As the student reads orally, mark any errors on your copy of the text. Stop the student at exactly one minute, and note precisely where the student stopped. Count the total number of words the student read in a minute. Subtract the number of words the student read incorrectly. Record the words correct per minute (WCPM) score on the Evaluation Chart.

Assess Comprehension Have the student reread the selection on page 19 quietly.

- **Now I want you to read the story selection to yourself.**
- **When you finish reading, I will ask you to tell me about what you read.**
- **Now read about finding information.**

When the student has finished, ask

- **What is this selection mostly about?**
- **What is important to know about finding information?**
- **What did you learn by reading this selection?**

Use the Expository Retelling Rubric that follows to evaluate the student's retelling. Record the Summative Score on the Evaluation Chart.

Summative Score Guidelines		
3 Rubric Score of all 3s in all Retelling Criteria	**2** Rubric Score of 3s, 2s, and some 1s in all Retelling Criteria	**1** Rubric Score of 1s or no response in all Retelling Criteria

Scoring Rubric Expository Retelling			
Score	**3**	**2**	**1**
Topic	Identifies the main topic with some details	Identifies the main topic with no details	Does not identify the main topic
Important Ideas	Identifies main ideas	Gives limited information about main ideas	Does not identify any main ideas or gives inaccurate information about ideas
Conclusions	Draws defensible conclusions about the text	Draws conclusions about the text with limited support	Draws inaccurate or no conclusions about the text

Note No score indicates no response.

4 Word Reading: Benchmark Words

This subtest should be given after Subtest 3 only to students who scored over 90% on Subtests 1–2 and who read and retold the Subtest 3 passage with a high degree of accuracy.

Display student test page 18. Say

- **Read the words in part 4 aloud. Begin next to the number 4, and read across the line. Read all four lines. Stop when you get to the end of part 4.**

Mark correct responses on your copy of the test page. Record the number correct on the Evaluation Chart. If the student scored 80% or better on Subtest 4, then ask the student to read Benchmark Reader D6 aloud. Use the Subtest 3 directions to evaluate the student's reading of Benchmark Reader D6.

1

ask	froze	spent	thinks	stripe
happens	plastic	problem	travel	children
strap	exhale	compute	inside	classmate
cities	planning	stopped	arrived	branches

2

listen	guess	heavy	worry	answer
instead	promise	though	usual	against
several	believe	certain	either	neighbor
minute	notice	company	thought	probably

3 Passage Reading

4

eleven	plumbing	couldn't	frequent	incomplete
disobey	icicle	suppose	microbe	lemonade
origin	cinnamon	nonprofit	certainly	announcement
knuckle	bankrupt	singular	diameter	refreshment

© Pearson Education E

Name _____ Date _____

Who won the World Series in 2005? What is the population   11

of India? Where was Abraham Lincoln born? You may not   21

know the answers to these questions off the top of your head,   33

but if you went on the Internet you could almost instantly find   45

the answers.   47

We live in an age of instant information. With the click of   59

a button you could find information on just about anything.   69

But wait! Is all of the information on the Internet correct? No!   81

The Internet is a great learning tool. Like any tool, you   92

have to know how to use it. Some Web sites have information   104

that is wrong. It could be a date. It could be a name. The only   119

way to really know whether the information is true or false   130

is to learn how to identify a reliable source. A reliable source   142

gives information that you can trust. A great way to learn   153

about reliable sources is to ask a teacher or a librarian.   164

Level E—Unit 1

My Sidewalks offers two assessment options for each unit: a one-on-one Individual Test and a Group Test. Use just one of these options with your students. The Individual Test is the preferred option for use with intervention students since it will give you more precise information about their reading skills. You do not need to administer both tests.

Option 1 Individual Test

Directions This test is to be administered one-on-one to individual students. Make two copies of the test on page 22 and of the fluency passage on page 25, one for the student and one for you to mark. Read aloud the directions in **bold**.

- **This is a test about reading. In the first part, you will read a selection aloud to me.**

Part One Fluency and Comprehension

Assess Fluency Take a one-minute sample of the student's oral reading of the passage on page 25.

- **I am going to ask you to read a selection aloud to me.**
- **Use your best reading as you read this selection titled "A Great Race."**

Have the student read aloud for one minute. Note miscues on your copy. After testing, record the words correct per minute (WCPM) on the Fluency Progress Chart on page 7.

Assess Comprehension Have the student read the story quietly. If the student has difficulty with the passage, you may read it aloud.

- **Now I want you to read the selection quietly to yourself.**
- **When you finish reading, I will ask you to tell me about what you read.**
- **Now read about the race.**

When the student has finished, or when you have finished reading it aloud, ask

- **What was the selection mostly about?**
- **What is important for you to know about the Iditarod?**
- **What did you learn from reading this selection?**

Use the Expository Retelling Rubric on page 8 to evaluate the student's retelling.

Part Two Phonics Words

Assess Phonics Skills Use the words at the top of page 22 to assess the student's ability to read words with this unit's phonics skills. Have each student read the words aloud. Mark errors on your copy. Record the student's score on the Word Reading Chart on page 30.

- **Now I'm going to ask you to read some words aloud to me.**
- **Point to the number one at the top of this page.**
- **Use your best reading to read the words in row 1.**

Continue in the same way for rows 2–5.

Part Three Phonics Sentences

Assess Phonics Skills Use the sentences in the middle of page 22 to assess the student's ability to read sentences with this unit's phonics skills. Have each student read the sentences aloud. Listen for the student's pronunciation of the phonics word in **bold** in each sentence. Mark errors on your copy. Record the student's score on the Word Reading Chart on page 30.

- **Now I'm going to ask you to read some sentences aloud to me.**
- **Point to the number six in the middle of this page.**
- **Use your best reading to read sentence 6.**

Continue in the same way for rows 7–10.

Part Four Concept Vocabulary

Assess Concept Vocabulary Use the words at the bottom of page 22 to assess the student's ability to read this unit's concept vocabulary. Have each student read the words aloud. Mark errors on your copy. Record the student's score on the Word Reading Chart on page 30.

- **Now I'm going to ask you to read some other words aloud to me.**
- **Point to the number eleven on this page.**
- **Use your best reading to read the words in row 11.**

Continue in the same way for rows 12–15.

Phonics Words

1. picnic   bandit   discuss   pumpkin   bathtub

2. suppose   pancake   mistake   expose   invite

3. bulbs   glasses   candies   plants   stretches

4. jumped   tricking   fishing   trotted   snagging

5. unhitch   unpack   dislike   nonstop   rename

Phonics Sentences

6. Kenneth made a jelly **sandwich** for lunch.

7. I have a problem, and I must get some **advice**.

8. Six **families** went camping with us.

9. Dennis **slipped** on the ice and fell.

10. Let's **recheck** the facts in this lesson one last time.

Concept Words

11. examination   challenge   chattered   volunteer   training

12. construct   design   damage   belongings   disaster

13. environment   wilderness   choices   compass   prepared

14. conquered   opponents   athlete   announcer   chance

15. cultures   ancestry   experience   nontraditional   unexpected

© Pearson Education E

Option 2 Group Test

Use this test if you prefer to assess in a group setting. Make copies of the test on pages 25–29 for each student. Since the Fluency and Comprehension test, which uses the passage on page 25, is to be administered individually, you will need two copies, one for the student to read and one for you to mark. Read aloud the directions in **bold**.

Part One Fluency and Comprehension

Assess Fluency Take a one-minute sample of the student's oral reading. This part of the test should be conducted with each student individually. Give the student a copy of the fluency passage "A Great Race" on page 25.

- **This is a test about reading.**
- **I am going to ask you to read a selection aloud to me.**
- **Use your best reading as you read this selection titled "A Great Race"**

Have the student read aloud for one minute. Note miscues on your copy. After testing, record the words correct per minute (WCPM) on the Fluency Progress Chart on page 7.

Assess Comprehension Have the student read the story quietly. If the student has difficulty with the passage, you may read it aloud.

- **Now I want you to read the selection quietly to yourself.**
- **When you finish reading, you will answer some questions about what you read.**
- **Now read about the race.**

When the student has finished, or when you have finished reading it aloud, say

- **Now look at page 26.**
- **Answer questions 1–5.**

(Possible answers to questions 1–5 may be found on page 92.)

Part Two Phonics Words

Make sure students are on page 27.

- **Now we are going to do something different.**
- **I will read a number and a word aloud.**
- **I will say each word twice. Fill in the circle under the word I say.**

Pause after each item to allow students time to mark their answers.

- **1. Fill in the circle under the word *discuss . . . discuss*.**
- **2. Fill in the circle under the word *suppose . . . suppose*.**
- **3. Fill in the circle under the word *punches . . . punches*.**
- **4. Fill in the circle under the word *trapping . . . trapping*.**
- **5. Fill in the circle under the word *unhappy . . . unhappy*.**

Record the student's score on the Word Reading Chart on page 31.

Part Three Phonics Sentences

Make sure the students are on page 28. Begin by saying

- **Now I will read a number and a sentence aloud.**

- **Follow along as I read each sentence. Then read the three words under the sentence.**

- **Find the word that best finishes the sentence.**

- **Fill in the circle next to the best word.**

- **Read the completed sentence aloud to me.**

Read the numbers and sentences below. Pause after each item to allow students time to mark their answers.

6. **Kenneth made a jelly . . . *blank* . . . for lunch. Fill in the circle next to your answer. Now read the sentence back to me.**

7. **I have a problem, and I need some . . . *blank.* Fill in the circle next to your answer. Now read the sentence back to me.**

8. **Six . . . *blank* . . . went camping with us. Fill in the circle next to your answer. Now read the sentence back to me.**

9. **Dennis . . . *blank* . . . on the ice and fell. Fill in the circle next to your answer. Now read the sentence back to me.**

10. **Let's . . . *blank* . . . the facts in this lesson one last time. Fill in the circle next to your answer. Now read the sentence back to me.**

Record the student's score on the Word Reading Chart on page 31.

Part Four Concept Vocabulary

Make sure the students are on page 29. Begin by saying

- **I will read a number and the definition of a word.**

- **Fill in the circle under the word that best matches the definition.**

Pause after each item to allow students time to mark their answers.

11. **Fill in the circle under the word that means a person who offers to help out or do a job.**

12. **Fill in the circle under the word that means to build or to put together.**

13. **Fill in the circle under the word that means a tool for finding directions.**

14. **Fill in the circle under the word that means people who are working against someone or something.**

15. **Fill in the circle under the word that means not in the usual way or not following the ideas of the people who came before.**

Record the student's score on the Word Reading Chart on page 31.

A Great Race

The crowd cheers as the dog sleds head into the   10

Alaskan wilderness. The Iditarod has begun! In the   18

coming weeks, the dog teams and their drivers will   27

compete against each other. They will also compete   35

against an even trickier opponent—nature.   41

The Iditarod is an annual race. It celebrates an   50

important event in Alaskan history. In 1925, dog   58

teams raced down the trail to deliver supplies of   67

lifesaving medicine to the people of Nome. Today's   75

racers run to experience the challenge. They face   83

harsh blizzards and jagged mountains. They cross   90

frozen rivers. They drive carefully through dense   97

forests. They cross miles of drifting snow on the   106

tundra.   107

The winners travel over 1000 miles in nine or ten   117

days. The losers may take more than two weeks.   126

There are no real losers in the Iditarod, though.   135

Everyone who competes in the race is a winner.   144

© Pearson Education E

Comprehension

Directions Answer the following questions about the passage you just read.

1. What is the Iditarod?

_____

_____

_____

2. What past event does the Iditarod celebrate?

_____

_____

_____

3. How is today's race like the one in 1925? How is it different?

_____

_____

_____

4. What challenges do racers face in the Iditarod?

_____

_____

_____

5. Why does the writer say there are no real losers in the Iditarod?

_____

_____

_____

Phonics Words

1. discuss   dispose   decide
   ○   ○   ○

2. suspect   supplies   suppose
   ○   ○   ○

3. punish   punches   puppies
   ○   ○   ○

4. trapping   traps   trapeze
   ○   ○   ○

5. happen   unhappy   happy
   ○   ○   ○

Phonics Sentences

6. Kenneth made a jelly _____ for lunch.

- ○ sands
- ○ sandwich
- ○ sandbag

7. I have a problem, and I need some _____.

- ○ revises
- ○ admit
- ○ advice

8. Six _____ went camping with us.

- ○ families
- ○ fishing
- ○ family

9. Dennis _____ on the ice and fell.

- ○ slaps
- ○ slipped
- ○ shopping

10. Let's _____ the facts in this lesson one last time.

- ○ nonstop
- ○ unpack
- ○ recheck

Name _____

Concept Words

11. athlete   announcer   volunteer

     ○   ○   ○

12. construct   design   damage

     ○   ○   ○

13. training   compass   belongings

     ○   ○   ○

14. cultures   wilderness   opponents

     ○   ○   ○

15. nontraditional   generation   experience

     ○   ○   ○

Student's Name _____

Word Reading Chart for Unit 1 Assessment

Administer the Individual Test or the Group Test, not both.

Test Option 1 — Individual Test				
Phonics Words Circle the items the student missed.	**Total Items**	**Items Correct**	**Reteach**	**Retest**
1. Closed syllables (VC/CV & VCCCV) with short vowels *picnic, bandit, discuss, pumpkin, bathtub*	5			
2. Closed syllables (VC/CV) with long vowels *suppose, pancake, mistake, expose, invite*	5			
3. Plurals and inflected endings -*s*, -*es*, -*ies*; spelling change: *y* to *i* *bulbs, glasses, candies, plants, stretches*	5			
4. Verb endings with and without spelling change: double final consonant *jumped, tricking, fishing, trotted, snagging*	5			
5. Prefixes *un-, dis-, non-, re-* *unhitch, unpack, dislike, nonstop, rename*	5			
Phonics Words Total	**25**			
Phonics Sentences	**Total Items**	**Words Correct**	**Reteach**	**Retest**
6. Closed syllables (VCCCV) with short vowels *sandwich*	1			
7. Closed syllables with long vowels *advice*	1			
8. Plurals and inflected endings -*ies*; spelling change: *y* to *i* *families*	1			
9. Verb endings with spelling change: double final consonant *slipped*	1			
10. Prefixes *re-* *recheck*	1			
Phonics Sentences Total	**5**			
Concept Vocabulary	**Total Items**	**Words Correct**	**Reteach**	**Retest**
11. *examination, challenge, chattered, volunteer, training*	5			
12. *construct, design, damage, belongings, disaster*	5			
13. *environment, wilderness, choices, compass, prepared*	5			
14. *conquered, opponents, athlete, announcer, chance*	5			
15. *cultures, ancestry, experience, nontraditional, unexpected*	5			
Concept Vocabulary Total	**25**			

© Pearson Education E

Word Reading Chart for Unit 1 Assessment

Administer the Individual Test or the Group Test, not both.

Test Option 2 — Group Test				
Phonics Words Items 1–10. Circle the items the student missed.	**Total Items**	**Items Correct**	**Reteach**	**Retest**
Closed syllables (VC/CV & VCCCV) with short vowels Items 1, 6	2			
Closed syllables (VC/CV) with long vowels Items 2, 7	2			
Plurals and inflected endings -es, -ies; spelling change: y to i Items 3, 8	2			
Verb endings with and without spelling change: double final consonant Items 4, 9	2			
Prefixes un-, re- Items 5, 10	2			
Phonics Words Total	**10**			
Concept Vocabulary Items 11–15	**Total Items**	**Items Correct**	**Reteach**	**Retest**
volunteer, construct, compass, opponents, nontraditional	5			
Concept Vocabulary Total	**5**			

- **RECORD SCORES** Use this chart to record scores.
- **RETEACH PHONICS SKILLS** If the student is unable to read words with particular phonics skills, then reteach the missed phonics skills.
- **PRACTICE CONCEPT VOCABULARY** If the student cannot read tested concept vocabulary, then provide additional practice.
- **RETEST** Use the same set of words or an alternate set for retesting.

Scores for Subtests: Individual/Group				
	Phonics		Concept Vocabulary	
	Ind.	Group	Ind.	Group
100%	30	10	25	5
80%	24	8	20	4
60%	18	6	15	3

Level E—Unit 2

My Sidewalks offers two assessment options for each unit: a one-on-one Individual Test and a Group Test. Use just one of these options with your students. The Individual Test is the preferred option for use with intervention students since it will give you more precise information about their reading skills. You do not need to administer both tests.

Option 1 Individual Test

Directions This test is to be administered one-on-one to individual students. Make two copies of the test on page 34 and of the fluency passage on page 37, one for the student and one for you to mark. Read aloud the directions in **bold**.

- **This is a test about reading. In the first part, you will read a selection aloud to me.**

Part One Fluency and Comprehension

Assess Fluency Take a one-minute sample of the student's oral reading of the passage on page 37.

- **I am going to ask you to read a selection aloud to me.**

- **Use your best reading as you read this selection titled "We're Here to Help!"**

Have the student read aloud for one minute. Note miscues on your copy. After testing, record the words correct per minute (WCPM) on the Fluency Progress Chart on page 7.

Assess Comprehension Have the student read the selection quietly. If the student has difficulty with the passage, you may read it aloud.

- **Now I want you to read the selection quietly to yourself.**

- **When you finish reading, I will ask you to tell me about what you read.**

- **Now read about people who help others.**

When the student has finished, or when you have finished reading it aloud, ask

- **What was the selection mostly about?**

- **What is important for you to know about people who help out after disasters?**

- **What did you learn from reading this selection?**

Use the Expository Retelling Rubric on page 8 to evaluate the student's retelling.

Part Two Phonics Words

Assess Phonics Skills Use the words at the top of page 34 to assess the student's ability to read words with this unit's phonics skills. Have each student read the words aloud. Mark errors on your copy. Record the student's score on the Word Reading Chart on page 42.

- **Now I'm going to ask you to read some words aloud to me.**

- **Point to the number one at the top of this page.**

- **Use your best reading to read the words in row 1.**

Continue in the same way for rows 2–5.

Part Three Phonics Sentences

Assess Phonics Skills Use the sentences in the middle of page 34 to assess the student's ability to read sentences with this unit's phonics skills. Have each student read the sentences aloud. Listen for the student's pronunciation of the phonics word in **bold** in each sentence. Mark errors on your copy. Record the student's score on the Word Reading Chart on page 42.

- **Now I'm going to ask you to read some sentences aloud to me.**
- **Point to the number six in the middle of this page.**
- **Use your best reading to read sentence 6.**

Continue in the same way for rows 7–10.

Part Four Concept Vocabulary

Assess Concept Vocabulary Use the words at the bottom of page 34 to assess the student's ability to read this unit's concept vocabulary. Have each student read the words aloud. Mark errors on your copy. Record the student's score on the Word Reading Chart on page 42.

- **Now I'm going to ask you to read some other words aloud to me.**
- **Point to the number eleven on this page.**
- **Use your best reading to read the words in row 11.**

Continue in the same way for rows 12–15.

Name _____

Phonics Words

1. carton   backyard   stork   forgot   explore

2. dirty   lantern   expert   church   surrender

3. closer   palest   drier   fluffier   sloppiest

4. protest   moment   pilot   dragon   profit

5. swiftly   useful   plentiful   divisible   dependable

Phonics Sentences

6. Martin's kitten **snores** when she takes a nap.

7. Kathy **hurried** to the barn with the horses before the storm hit.

8. When I am sad, music makes me feel **happier**.

9. Kevin saw a baby **robin** in the nest.

10. My sister is **thankful** when I help in the garden.

Concept Words

11. intrinsic   considerate   charity   organization   fortunate

12. beneficial   courageous   emergency   intervene   excursion

13. distress   panic   assistance   relief   improve

14. naturalist   wildlife   mission   human   donate

15. battles   freedom   equality   guarantee   intolerable

Option 2 Group Test

Use this test if you prefer to assess in a group setting. Make copies of the test on pages 37–41 for each student. Since the Fluency and Comprehension test, which uses the passage on page 37, is to be administered individually, you will need two copies, one for the student to read and one for you to mark. Read aloud the directions in **bold**.

Part One Fluency and Comprehension

Assess Fluency Take a one-minute sample of the student's oral reading. Note miscues on your copy. This part of the test should be conducted with each student individually. Give the student a copy of the fluency passage "We're Here to Help!" on page 37.

- **This is a test about reading.**
- **I am going to ask you to read a selection aloud to me.**
- **Use your best reading as you read this selection titled "We're Here to Help!"**

Have the student read aloud for one minute. Note miscues on your copy. After testing, record the words correct per minute (WCPM) on the Fluency Progress Chart on page 7.

Assess Comprehension Have the student read the selection quietly. If the student has difficulty with the passage, you may read it aloud.

- **Now I want you to read the selection quietly to yourself.**
- **When you finish reading, you will answer some questions about what you read.**
- **Now read about people who help others.**

When the student has finished, or when you have finished reading it aloud, say

- **Now look at page 38.**
- **Answer questions 1–5.**

(Possible answers to questions 1–5 may be found on page 92.)

Part Two Phonics Words

Make sure students are on page 39.

- **Now we are going to do something different.**
- **I will read a number and a word aloud.**
- **I will say each word twice. Fill in the circle under the word I say.**

Pause after each item to allow students time to mark their answers.

1. **Fill in the circle under the word** *darken . . . darken.*
2. **Fill in the circle under the word** *squirting . . . squirting.*
3. **Fill in the circle under the word** *safer . . . safer.*
4. **Fill in the circle under the word** *profile . . . profile.*
5. **Fill in the circle under the word** *suddenly . . . suddenly.*

Record the student's score on the Word Reading Chart on page 43.

© Pearson Education E

Part Three Phonics Sentences

Make sure the students are on page 40. Begin by saying

- **Now I will read a number and a sentence aloud.**
- **Follow along as I read each sentence. Then read the three words under the sentence.**
- **Find the word that best finishes the sentence.**
- **Fill in the circle next to the best word.**
- **Read the completed sentence aloud to me.**

Read the numbers and sentences below. Pause after each item to allow students time to mark their answers.

6. **Martin's kitten . . . *blank* . . . when she takes a nap. Fill in the circle next to your answer. Now read the sentence back to me.**

7. **Kathy . . . *blank* . . . to the stable with the horses before the storm hit. Fill in the circle next to your answer. Now read the sentence back to me.**

8. **My sister got the . . . *blank* . . . of all the kids on Sports Day. Fill in the circle next to your answer. Now read the sentence back to me.**

9. **Kevin saw a baby . . . *blank* . . . in the nest. Fill in the circle next to your answer. Now read the sentence back to me.**

10. **My sister is . . . *blank* . . . when I help in the garden. Fill in the circle next to your answer. Now read the sentence back to me.**

Record the student's score on the Word Reading Chart on page 43.

Part Four Concept Vocabulary

Make sure the students are on page 41. Begin by saying

- **I will read a number and the definition of a word.**
- **Fill in the circle under the word that best matches the definition.**

Pause after each item to allow students time to mark their answers.

11. **Fill in the circle under the word that means careful to think about the feelings and the well-being of others.**

12. **Fill in the circle under the word that means brave.**

13. **Fill in the circle under the word that means to make better.**

14. **Fill in the circle under the word that means having to do with people.**

15. **Fill in the circle under the word that means promise.**

Record the student's score on the Word Reading Chart on page 43.

We're Here to Help!

A devastating tornado just roared through town.　　　7

It's the middle of the night. The people in the　　　17

tornado's path are frightened and in shock. They　　　25

need help right away. Already phones are ringing in　　　34

the homes of nearby disaster relief volunteers. The　　　42

volunteers leap out of bed and drive into the night.　　　52

Who are these ever ready volunteers? They're　　　59

people just like you and me. They have a desire to　　　70

help and are flexible enough to rearrange their lives　　　79

in a minute. They also have training that helps them　　　89

think on their feet in even the scariest emergency.　　　98

Soon the volunteers are pouring into the　　　105

devastated area. They bring urgently needed　　　111

supplies. They jump right into action to offer　　　119

assistance and support to the shaken people. And　　　127

right away, the storm victims know the situation is　　　136

starting to improve. They are reassured when they　　　144

hear the words, "We're here to help."　　　151

Comprehension

Directions Answer the following questions about the passage you just read.

1. What are disaster relief volunteers?

_____

_____

_____

2. What happens after a tornado or another disaster occurs?

_____

_____

_____

3. How do you think the volunteers are like you? How do you think they are different?

_____

_____

_____

4. What kinds of supplies would the volunteers probably bring?

_____

_____

_____

5. How do victims feel just after the disaster? How do many victims feel after the volunteers arrive?

_____

_____

_____

Phonics Words

1.   darken   during   dangle

         ○   ○   ○

2.   square   squirting   scoring

         ○   ○   ○

3.   safer   safest   safely

         ○   ○   ○

4.   perfect   profit   profile

         ○   ○   ○

5.   sorrowful   sellable   suddenly

         ○   ○   ○

Phonics Sentences

6. Martin's kitten _____ when she takes a nap.

   ○ snows

   ○ snores

   ○ snacks

7. Kathy _____ to the stable with the horses before the storm hit.

   ○ hurried

   ○ hardly

   ○ helpful

8. My sister got the _____ of all the kids on Sports Day.

   ○ muddiest

   ○ muddy

   ○ happier

9. Kevin saw a baby _____ in the nest.

   ○ robber

   ○ robin

   ○ robot

10. My sister is _____ when I help in the garden.

   ○ thankful

   ○ possible

   ○ nicely

© Pearson Education E

Name _____

Concept Words

11.   intrinsic   fortunate   considerate
     ○   ○   ○

12.   courageous   beneficial   intervene
     ○   ○   ○

13.   distress   improve   relief
     ○   ○   ○

14.   human   mission   donate
     ○   ○   ○

15.   intolerable   equality   guarantee
     ○   ○   ○

Student's Name _____

Word Reading Chart for Unit 2 Assessment

Administer the Individual Test or the Group Test, not both.

Test Option 1 — Individual Test				
Phonics Words Circle the items the student missed.	**Total Items**	**Items Correct**	**Reteach**	**Retest**
1. Syllables with *r*-controlled *ar, or, ore* carton, backyard, stork, forgot, explore	5			
2. Syllables with *r*-controlled *er, ir, ur* dirty, lantern, expert, church, surrender	5			
3. Endings *-er, -est;* spelling change: drop *e* and *y* to *i* closer, palest, drier, fluffier, sloppiest	5			
4. Open and closed syllables protest, moment, pilot, dragon, profit	5			
5. Suffixes *-ly, -ful, -able, -ible* swiftly, useful, plentiful, divisible, dependable	5			
Phonics Words Total	**25**			
Phonics Sentences	**Total Items**	**Words Correct**	**Reteach**	**Retest**
6. Syllables with *r*-controlled *ore* snores	1			
7. Syllables with *r*-controlled *ur* hurried	1			
8. Endings *-er,* spelling change: change *y* to *i* happier	1			
9. Closed syllables robin	1			
10. Suffix *-ful* thankful	1			
Phonics Sentences Total	**5**			
Concept Vocabulary	**Total Items**	**Words Correct**	**Reteach**	**Retest**
11. *intrinsic, considerate, charity, organization, fortunate*	5			
12. *beneficial, courageous, emergency, intervene, excursion*	5			
13. *distress, panic, assistance, relief, improve*	5			
14. *naturalist, wildlife, mission, human, donate*	5			
15. *battles, freedom, equality, guarantee, intolerable*	5			
Concept Vocabulary Total	**25**			

Word Reading Chart for Unit 2 Assessment

Administer the Individual Test or the Group Test, not both.

Test Option 2 — Group Test				
Phonics Words Items 1–10. Circle the items the student missed.	**Total Items**	**Items Correct**	**Reteach**	**Retest**
Syllables with *r*-controlled *ar, or* Items 1, 6	2			
Syllables with *r*-controlled *ir, ur* Items 2, 7	2			
Endings *-er, -est*; spelling change: drop *e* and *y* to *i* Items 3, 8	2			
Open and closed syllables Items 4, 9	2			
Suffixes *-ful, -ly* Items 5, 10	2			
Phonics Words Total	**10**			
Concept Vocabulary Items 11–15	**Total Items**	**Items Correct**	**Reteach**	**Retest**
considerate, courageous, improve, human, guarantee	5			
Concept Vocabulary Total	**5**			

- **RECORD SCORES** Use this chart to record scores.
- **RETEACH PHONICS SKILLS** If the student is unable to read words with particular phonics skills, then reteach the missed phonics skills.
- **PRACTICE CONCEPT VOCABULARY** If the student cannot read tested concept vocabulary, then provide additional practice.
- **RETEST** Use the same set of words or an alternate set for retesting.

Scores for Subtests: Individual/Group				
	Phonics		Vocabulary	
	Ind.	Group	Ind.	Group
100%	30	10	25	5
80%	24	8	20	4
60%	18	6	15	3

Level E—Unit 3

My Sidewalks offers two assessment options for each unit: a one-on-one Individual Test and a Group Test. Use just one of these options with your students. The Individual Test is the preferred option for use with intervention students since it will give you more precise information about their reading skills. You do not need to administer both tests.

Option 1 Individual Test

Directions This test is to be administered one-on-one to individual students. Make two copies of the test on page 46 and of the fluency passage on page 49, one for the student and one for you to mark. Read aloud the directions in **bold**.

- **This is a test about reading. In the first part, you will read a selection aloud to me.**

Part One Fluency and Comprehension

Assess Fluency Take a one-minute sample of the student's oral reading of the passage on page 49.

- **I am going to ask you to read a selection aloud to me.**
- **Use your best reading as you read this selection titled "*Mona Lisa*'s Secret."**

Have the student read aloud for one minute. Note miscues on your copy. After testing, record the words correct per minute (WCPM) on the Fluency Progress Chart on page 7.

Assess Comprehension Have the student read the selection quietly. If the student has difficulty with the passage, you may read it aloud.

- **Now I want you to read the selection quietly to yourself.**
- **When you finish reading, I will ask you to tell me about what you read.**
- **Now read about the *Mona Lisa*.**

When the student has finished, or when you have finished reading it aloud, ask

- **What was the selection mostly about?**
- **What is important for you to know about the *Mona Lisa*?**
- **What did you learn from reading this selection?**

Use the Expository Retelling Rubric on page 8 to evaluate the student's retelling.

Part Two Phonics Words

Assess Phonics Skills Use the words at the top of page 46 to assess the student's ability to read words with this unit's phonics skills. Have each student read the words aloud. Mark errors on your copy. Record the student's score on the Word Reading Chart on page 54.

- **Now I'm going to ask you to read some words aloud to me.**
- **Point to the number one at the top of this page.**
- **Use your best reading to read the words in row 1.**

Continue in the same way for rows 2–5.

Part Three Phonics Sentences

Assess Phonics Skills Use the sentences in the middle of page 46 to assess the student's ability to read sentences with this unit's phonics skills. Have each student read the sentences aloud. Listen for the student's pronunciation of the phonics word in **bold** in each sentence. Mark errors on your copy. Record the student's score on the Word Reading Chart on page 54.

- **Now I'm going to ask you to read some sentences aloud to me.**
- **Point to the number six in the middle of this page.**
- **Use your best reading to read sentence 6.**

Continue in the same way for rows 7–10.

Part Four Concept Vocabulary

Assess Concept Vocabulary Use the words at the bottom of page 46 to assess the student's ability to read this unit's concept vocabulary. Have each student read the words aloud. Mark errors on your copy. Record the student's score on the Word Reading Chart on page 54.

- **Now I'm going to ask you to read some other words aloud to me.**
- **Point to the number eleven on this page.**
- **Use your best reading to read the words in row 11.**

Continue in the same way for rows 12–15.

Phonics Words

1. replay   castaway   painful   maintain   proclaim

2. we   sweeten   sneeze   increase   reasoning

3. doesn't   I've   you'll   don't   won't

4. elbow   borrow   lower   toaster   cockroach

5. illegal   invisible   irregular   imperfect   impossible

Phonics Sentences

6. Dad loaded the paint cans into the **trailer**.

7. Kelly asked for three slices of **cheese** on her sandwich.

8. **We'll** hike on the forest trail as soon as it stops raining.

9. He **groaned** when Mr. Blain asked him to mow the yard.

10. It's **illogical** to begin building without reading the plans.

Concept Words

11. experiment   theory   evaluate   brainstorm   brilliant

12. canvas   style   murals   gallery   famous

13. excavate   prehistoric   sites   extinct   paleontologists

14. instrument   harmony   concert   fiddle   studio

15. effects   illusions   theater   audience   broadcast

Option 2 Group Test

Use this test if you prefer to assess in a group setting. Make copies of the test on pages 49–53 for each student. Since the Fluency and Comprehension test, which uses the passage on page 49, is to be administered individually, you will need two copies, one for the student to read and one for you to mark. Read aloud the directions in **bold**.

Part One Fluency and Comprehension

Assess Fluency Take a one-minute sample of the student's oral reading. This part of the test should be conducted with each student individually. Give the student a copy of the fluency passage "*Mona Lisa*'s Secret" on page 49.

- **This is a test about reading.**
- **I am going to ask you to read a selection aloud to me.**
- **Use your best reading as you read this selection titled "*Mona Lisa*'s Secret."**

Have the student read aloud for one minute. Note miscues on your copy. After testing, record the words correct per minute (WCPM) on the Fluency Progress Chart on page 7.

Assess Comprehension Have the student read the selection quietly. If the student has difficulty with the passage, you may read it aloud.

- **Now I want you to read the selection quietly to yourself.**
- **When you finish reading, you will answer some questions about what you read.**
- **Now read about the *Mona Lisa*.**

When the student has finished, or when you have finished reading it aloud, say

- **Now look at page 50.**
- **Answer questions 1–5.**

(Possible answers to questions 1–5 may be found on page 92.)

Part Two Phonics Words

Make sure students are on page 51.

- **Now we are going to do something different.**
- **I will read a number and a word aloud.**
- **I will say each word twice. Fill in the circle under the word I say.**

Pause after each item to allow students time to mark their answers.

1. **Fill in the circle under the word *replay* . . . *replay*.**
2. **Fill in the circle under the word *streak* . . . *streak*.**
3. **Fill in the circle under the word *doesn't* . . . *doesn't*.**
4. **Fill in the circle under the word *follow* . . . *follow*.**
5. **Fill in the circle under the word *improper* . . . *improper*.**

Record the student's score on the Word Reading Chart on page 55.

Part Three Phonics Sentences

Make sure the students are on page 52. Begin by saying

- **Now I will read a number and a sentence aloud.**
- **Follow along as I read each sentence. Then read the three words under the sentence.**
- **Find the word that best finishes the sentence.**
- **Fill in the circle next to the best word.**
- **Read the completed sentence aloud to me.**

Read the numbers and sentences below. Pause after each item to allow students time to mark their answers.

6. **Dad loaded the paint cans into the . . . *blank*. Fill in the circle next to your answer. Now read the sentence back to me.**

7. **Kelly asked for three slices of . . . *blank* . . . on her sandwich. Fill in the circle next to your answer. Now read the sentence back to me.**

8. ***Blank* . . . hike on the forest trail as soon as it stops raining. Fill in the circle next to your answer. Now read the sentence back to me.**

9. **He . . . *blank* . . . when Mr. Blain asked him to mow the yard. Fill in the circle next to your answer. Now read the sentence back to me.**

10. **It's . . . *blank* . . . to begin building without reading the plans. Fill in the circle next to your answer. Now read the sentence back to me.**

Record the student's score on the Word Reading Chart on page 55.

Part Four Concept Vocabulary

Make sure the students are on page 53. Begin by saying

- **I will read a number and the definition of a word.**
- **Fill in the circle under the word that best matches the definition.**

Pause after each item to allow students time to mark their answers.

11. **Fill in the circle under the word that means an idea that has not yet been proved.**

12. **Fill in the circle under the word that means large pictures painted on walls.**

13. **Fill in the circle under the word that means to dig up or unearth.**

14. **Fill in the circle under the word that means a place where musicians play and record songs.**

15. **Fill in the circle under the word that means a group of people who watch or listen to a show or performance.**

Record the student's score on the Word Reading Chart on page 55.

© Pearson Education E

Mona Lisa's Secret

Some consider the *Mona Lisa* to be the world's   9

greatest painting, and it is certainly the best known.   18

Viewers spend hours studying *Mona Lisa*'s sly   25

smile. Maybe she's smiling because she can keep   33

secrets. She won't tell about her mysterious theft.   41

In 1911, the painting was taken from its site in   51

the Louvre Museum in Paris. At first, no one even   61

reported it missing. Everyone thought it had been   69

removed for official reasons. It had really been   77

stolen by a worker who hid in the museum after it   88

closed. The thief cut the canvas out of the frame and   99

then escaped by unscrewing a doorknob. The   106

painting was gone for about two years. The theft   115

had a frightening effect on the art world until   124

someone came up with a brilliant idea. Today the   133

Mona Lisa is locked in a bulletproof glass box. It is   144

easy to view but impossible to steal, and that's a   154

very good thing. The *Mona Lisa* is irreplaceable.   162

Comprehension

Directions Answer the following questions about the passage you just read.

1. What is the *Mona Lisa*?

_____

_____

2. What big event happened to the *Mona Lisa* in 1911?

_____

_____

_____

3. Why do you think the thief cut the canvas out of its frame?

_____

_____

_____

4. The *Mona Lisa* is displayed differently now than it was in 1911. What has changed?

_____

_____

_____

5. Why is bulletproof glass a good material to use in protecting the painting?

_____

_____

_____

© Pearson Education E

Phonics Words

1. replan   replay   repeat

○   ○   ○

2. stretch   stress   streak

○   ○   ○

3. doesn't   don't   didn't

○   ○   ○

4. forest   follow   flower

○   ○   ○

5. illegal   improper   interesting

○   ○   ○

Phonics Sentences

6. Dad loaded the paint cans into the _____.

- ○ trapper
- ○ taller
- ○ trailer

7. Kelly asked for three slices of _____ on her sandwich.

- ○ cheats
- ○ cheese
- ○ she's

8. _____ hike on the forest trail as soon as it stops raining.

- ○ We'll
- ○ We're
- ○ We've

9. He _____ when Mr. Blain asked him to mow the yard.

- ○ groaned
- ○ grown
- ○ grain

10. It's _____ to begin building without reading the plans.

- ○ immune
- ○ inactive
- ○ illogical

Name _____

Concept Words

11.   experiment   theory   evaluate

             ○   ○   ○

12.   canvas   gallery   murals

             ○   ○   ○

13.   excavate   extinct   paleontologists

             ○   ○   ○

14.   harmony   concert   studio

             ○   ○   ○

15.   audience   illusions   theater

             ○   ○   ○

© Pearson Education E

Word Reading Chart for Unit 3 Assessment

Administer the Individual Test or the Group Test, not both.

Test Option 1 — Individual Test				
Phonics Words Circle the items the student missed.	**Total Items**	**Items Correct**	**Reteach**	**Retest**
1. Syllables with long *a* spelled *ai, ay* *replay, castaway, painful, maintain, proclaim*	5			
2. Syllables with long *e* spelled *e, ee, ea* *we, sweeten, sneeze, increase, reasoning*	5			
3 Contractions *doesn't, I've, you'll, don't, won't*	5			
4. Syllables with long *o* spelled *oa, ow* *elbow, borrow, lower, toaster, cockroach*	5			
5. Prefixes *il-, in-, ir- im-* *illegal, invisible, irregular, imperfect, impossible*	5			
Phonics Words Total	**25**			
Phonics Sentences	**Total Items**	**Words Correct**	**Reteach**	**Retest**
6. Syllables with long *a* spelled *ai* *trailer*	1			
7. Syllables with long *e* spelled *ee* *cheese*	1			
8. Contractions *we'll*	1			
9. Syllables with long *o* spelled *oa* *groaned*	1			
10. Prefix *il-* *illogical*	1			
Phonics Sentences Total	**5**			
Concept Vocabulary	**Total Items**	**Words Correct**	**Reteach**	**Retest**
11. *experiment, theory, evaluate, brainstorm, brilliant*	5			
12. *canvas, style, murals, gallery, famous*	5			
13. *excavate, prehistoric, sites, extinct, paleontologists*	5			
14. *instrument, harmony, concert, fiddle, studio*	5			
15. *effects, illusions, theater, audience, broadcast*	5			
Concept Vocabulary Total	**25**			

Word Reading Chart for Unit 3 Assessment

Administer the Individual Test or the Group Test, not both.

Test Option 2 — Group Test				
Phonics Words Items 1–10. Circle the items the student missed.	**Total Items**	**Items Correct**	**Reteach**	**Retest**
Syllables with long *a* spelled *ai, ay* Items 1, 6	2			
Syllables with long *e* spelled *ee, ea* Items 2, 7	2			
Contractions Items 3, 8	2			
Syllables with long *o* spelled *oa, ow* Items 4, 9	2			
Prefixes *im-, il-* Items 5, 10	2			
Phonics Words Total	**10**			
Concept Vocabulary Items 11–15	**Total Items**	**Items Correct**	**Reteach**	**Retest**
theory, murals, excavate, studio, audience	5			
Concept Vocabulary Total	**5**			

- **RECORD SCORES** Use this chart to record scores.
- **RETEACH PHONICS SKILLS** If the student is unable to read words with particular phonics skills, then reteach the missed phonics skills.
- **PRACTICE CONCEPT VOCABULARY** If the student cannot read tested concept vocabulary, then provide additional practice.
- **RETEST** Use the same set of words or an alternate set for retesting.

Scores for Subtests: Individual/Group				
	Phonics		Vocabulary	
	Ind.	Group	Ind.	Group
100%	30	10	25	5
80%	24	8	20	4
60%	18	6	15	3

Level E—Unit 4

My Sidewalks offers two assessment options for each unit: a one-on-one Individual Test and a Group Test. Use just one of these options with your students. The Individual Test is the preferred option for use with intervention students since it will give you more precise information about their reading skills. You do not need to administer both tests.

Option 1 Individual Test

Directions This test is to be administered one-on-one to individual students. Make two copies of the test on page 58 and of the fluency passage on page 61, one for the student and one for you to mark. Read aloud the directions in **bold**.

- **This is a test about reading. In the first part, you will read a story aloud to me.**

Part One Fluency and Comprehension

Assess Fluency Take a one-minute sample of the student's oral reading of the passage on page 61.

- **I am going to ask you to read a story aloud to me.**
- **Use your best reading as you read this story titled "The Educated Monkey."**

Have the student read aloud for one minute. Note miscues on your copy. After testing, record the words correct per minute (WCPM) on the Fluency Progress Chart on page 7.

Assess Comprehension Have the student read the story quietly. If the student has difficulty with the passage, you may read it aloud.

- **Now I want you to read the story quietly to yourself.**
- **When you finish reading, I will ask you to tell me about what you read.**
- **Now read about Minnie the monkey.**

When the student has finished, or when you have finished reading it aloud, ask

- **Who is Minnie? Who is Mike? Tell me more about them.**
- **Where or when does the story take place?**
- **What is the problem or goal? How is the problem solved or the goal reached?**

Use the Narrative Retelling Rubric on page 8 to evaluate the student's retelling.

Part Two Phonics Words

Assess Phonics Skills Use the words at the top of page 58 to assess the student's ability to read words with this unit's phonics skills. Have each student read the words aloud. Record the student's score on the Word Reading Chart on page 66.

- **Now I'm going to ask you to read some words aloud to me.**
- **Point to the number one at the top of this page.**
- **Use your best reading to read the words in row 1.**

Continue in the same way for rows 2–5.

Part Three Phonics Sentences

Assess Phonics Skills Use the sentences in the middle of page 58 to assess the student's ability to read sentences with this unit's phonics skills. Have each student read the sentences aloud. Listen for the student's pronunciation of the phonics word in **bold** in each sentence. Mark errors on your copy. Record the student's score on the Word Reading Chart on page 66.

- **Now I'm going to ask you to read some sentences aloud to me.**
- **Point to the number six in the middle of this page.**
- **Use your best reading to read sentence 6.**

Continue in the same way for rows 7–10.

Part Four Concept Vocabulary

Assess Concept Vocabulary Use the words at the bottom of page 58 to assess the student's ability to read this unit's concept vocabulary. Have each student read the words aloud. Mark errors on your copy. Record the student's score on the Word Reading Chart on page 66.

- **Now I'm going to ask you to read some other words aloud to me.**
- **Point to the number eleven on this page.**
- **Use your best reading to read the words in row 11.**

Continue in the same way for rows 12–15.

Name _____

Phonics Words

1. driveway   sandpaper   daydream   horseback   grasshopper

2. untie   sky   reply   fright   lightning

3. noble   title   chuckle   grumble   twinkle

4. stout   founder   crouch   powder   shower

5. musical   personal   athletic   historic   familial

Phonics Sentences

6. Mr. Brown rode a **skateboard** downtown.

7. David painted the walls yellow to **brighten** the room.

8. The baby slept soundly in the **cradle**.

9. I was **grouchy** because the rainstorm ended our game.

10. Jenny's fine sketches show that she is quite **artistic**.

Concept Words

11. congestion   urban   rural   potential   salvage

12. rehabilitation   physical   successful   confidently   persist

13. transform   domesticated   feral   nurture   camouflage

14. adjust   modify   accustomed   architect   evolved

15. motivation   nutrition   exercise   principles   discipline

Option 2 Group Test

Use this test if you prefer to assess in a group setting. Make copies of the test on pages 61–65 for each student. Since the Fluency and Comprehension test, which uses the passage on page 61, is to be administered individually, you will need two copies, one for the student to read and one for you to mark. Read aloud the directions in **bold**.

Part One Fluency and Comprehension

Assess Fluency Take a one-minute sample of the student's oral reading. Note miscues on your copy. This part of the test should be conducted with each student individually. Give the student a copy of the fluency passage "The Educated Monkey" on page 61.

- **This is a test about reading.**
- **I am going to ask you to read a story aloud to me.**
- **Use your best reading as you read this story titled "The Educated Monkey."**

Have the student read aloud for one minute. Note miscues on your copy. After testing, record the words correct per minute (wcpm) on the Fluency Progress Chart on page 7.

Assess Comprehension Have the student read the story quietly. If the student has difficulty with the passage, you may read it aloud.

- **Now I want you to read the story quietly to yourself.**
- **When you finish reading, you will answer some questions about what you read.**
- **Now read about Minnie the monkey.**

When the student has finished, or when you have finished reading it aloud, say

- **Now look at page 62.**
- **Answer questions 1–5.**

(Possible answers to questions 1–5 may be found on page 93.)

Part Two Phonics Words

Make sure students are on page 63.

- **Now we are going to do something different.**
- **I will read a number and a word aloud.**
- **I will say each word twice. Fill in the circle under the word I say.**

Pause after each item to allow students time to mark their answers.

1. **Fill in the circle under the word *handshake* . . . *handshake.***
2. **Fill in the circle under the word *reply* . . . *reply.***
3. **Fill in the circle under the word *grumble* . . . *grumble.***
4. **Fill in the circle under the word *prowler* . . . *prowler.***
5. **Fill in the circle under the word *coastal* . . . *coastal.***

Record the student's score on the Word Reading Chart on page 67.

Part Three Phonics Sentences

Make sure the students are on page 64. Begin by saying

- **Now I will read a number and a sentence aloud.**

- **Follow along as I read each sentence. Then read the three words under the sentence.**

- **Find the word that best finishes the sentence.**

- **Fill in the circle next to the best word.**

- **Read the completed sentence aloud to me.**

Read the numbers and sentences below. Pause after each item to allow students time to mark their answers.

6. **Mr. Brown rode a . . . *blank* . . . downtown. Fill in the circle next to your answer. Now read the sentence back to me.**

7. **David painted the walls yellow to . . . *blank* . . . the room. Fill in the circle next to your answer. Now read the sentence back to me.**

8. **The baby slept soundly in the . . . *blank*. Fill in the circle next to your answer. Now read the sentence back to me.**

9. **I was . . . *blank* . . . because the rainstorm ended our game. Fill in the circle next to your answer. Now read the sentence back to me.**

10. **Jenny's fine sketches show that she is quite . . . *blank*. Fill in the circle next to your answer. Now read the sentence back to me.**

Record the student's score on the Word Reading Chart on page 67.

Part Four Concept Vocabulary

Make sure the students are on page 65. Begin by saying

- **I will read a number and the definition of a word.**

- **Fill in the circle under the word that best matches the definition.**

Pause after each item to allow students time to mark their answers.

11. **Fill in the circle under the word that means having to do with a city or with city life.**

12. **Fill in the circle under the word that means to endure or to keep trying when someone or something is trying to stop you.**

13. **Fill in the circle under the word that means to take care of, or to protect, support, and encourage.**

14. **Fill in the circle under the word that means to change slightly.**

15. **Fill in the circle under the word that means the ideas or rules that guide how a person or group of people behaves.**

Record the student's score on the Word Reading Chart on page 67.

© Pearson Education E

Name _____

The Educated Monkey

The accident changed Mike's life in the blink of   9

an eye. The resulting physical disability transformed   16

everyday tasks into challenges. Now that he used a   25

wheelchair, turning on overhead lights or getting a   33

box from a high shelf was a struggle. Then Mike   43

found out he could get a personal assistant. The big   53

surprise was that his assistant would be a monkey!   62

Mike's therapist Pam arrived at Mike's office with a   71

tame monkey named Minnie. Mike giggled when the spry   80

little monkey leaped down and ran around his chair.   89

Minnie had already completed "monkey college."   95

She knew how to turn on a computer. She could   105

pick up dropped objects. Now Mike had to learn to   115

work with her. Pam taught Mike some simple   123

commands. She demonstrated how to use a laser   131

pointer to show Minnie which objects to get. Mike   140

and Minnie agreed to adopt each other. Now they   149

both have a new lifestyle and a new lifelong friend.   159

Comprehension

Directions Answer the following questions about the passage you just read.

1. What was Mike's problem at the beginning of the story?

_____

_____

2. Who was Minnie?

_____

_____

3. What kinds of things did Minnie learn at "monkey college"?

_____

_____

4. How was Minnie like a human assistant? How was she different?

_____

_____

_____

5. Do you think Mike was happy that his assistant turned out to be a monkey? Why do think as you do?

_____

_____

_____

Name _____

Phonics Words

1. handshake   headstrong   happily
    ○   ○   ○

2. return   reply   replayed
    ○   ○   ○

3. grunted   grumble   jingle
    ○   ○   ○

4. proud   powder   prowler
    ○   ○   ○

5. coastal   coastline   coattail
    ○   ○   ○

Phonics Sentences

6. Mr. Brown rode a _____ downtown.

  ○ boathouse

  ○ skateboard

  ○ blackboard

7. David painted the walls yellow to _____ the room.

  ○ brighten

  ○ daylight

  ○ might

8. The baby slept soundly in the _____.

  ○ candle

  ○ cradle

  ○ cable

9. I was _____ because the rainstorm ended our game.

  ○ flounder

  ○ slouch

  ○ grouchy

10. Jenny's fine sketches show that she is quite _____.

  ○ artistic

  ○ athletic

  ○ dreamland

© Pearson Education E

Concept Words

11. urban rural congestion

        ○   ○   ○

12. confidently persist successful

        ○   ○   ○

13. domesticated evolved nurture

        ○   ○   ○

14. transform accustomed modify

        ○   ○   ○

15. motivation principles exercise

        ○   ○   ○

Word Reading Chart for Unit 4 Assessment

Administer the Individual Test or the Group Test, not both.

Test Option 1 — Individual Test				
Phonics Words Circle the items the student missed.	**Total Items**	**Items Correct**	**Reteach**	**Retest**
1. Compound words *driveway, sandpaper, daydream, horseback, grasshopper*	5			
2. Syllables with long *i* spelled *igh, ie,* final *y* *untie, sky, reply, fright, lightning*	5			
3. Consonant + *le* syllables (open and closed) *noble, title, chuckle, grumble, twinkle*	5			
4. Syllables with diphthongs *ou, ow /ou/* *stout, founder, crouch, powder, shower*	5			
5. Suffixes *-al, -ial, -ic* *musical, personal, athletic, historic, familial*	5			
Phonics Words Total	**25**			
Phonics Sentences	**Total Items**	**Words Correct**	**Reteach**	**Retest**
6. Compound words *skateboard*	1			
7. Syllables with long *i* spelled *igh* brighten	1			
8. Consonant + *le* syllables *cradle*	1			
9. Syllables with diphthongs *ou /ou/* *grouchy*	1			
10. Suffixes *-ic* *artistic*	1			
Phonics Sentences Total	**5**			
Concept Vocabulary	**Total Items**	**Words Correct**	**Reteach**	**Retest**
11. *congestion, urban, rural, potential, salvage*	5			
12. *rehabilitation, physical, successful, confidently, persist*	5			
13. *transform, domesticated, feral, nurture, camouflage*	5			
14. *adjust, modify, accustomed, architect, evolved*	5			
15. *motivation, nutrition, exercise, principles, discipline*	5			
Concept Vocabulary Total	**25**			

Word Reading Chart for Unit 4 Assessment

Administer the Individual Test or the Group Test, not both.

Test Option 2 — Group Test				
Phonics Words Items 1–10. Circle the items the student missed.	**Total Items**	**Items Correct**	**Reteach**	**Retest**
Compound words Items 1, 6	2			
Syllables with long *i* spelled *igh, ie,* final *y* Items 2, 7	2			
Consonants + *le* syllables (open and closed) Items 3, 8	2			
Syllables with diphthongs *ou, ow /ou/* Items 4, 9	2			
Suffixes *-al, -ial, -ic* Items 5, 10	2			
Phonics Words Total	**10**			
Concept Vocabulary Items 11–15	**Total Items**	**Items Correct**	**Reteach**	**Retest**
urban, persist, nurture, modify, principles	5			
Concept Vocabulary Total	**5**			

- **RECORD SCORES** Use this chart to record scores.
- **RETEACH PHONICS SKILLS** If the student is unable to read words with particular phonics skills, then reteach the missed phonics skills.
- **PRACTICE CONCEPT VOCABULARY** If the student cannot read tested concept vocabulary, then provide additional practice.
- **RETEST** Use the same set of words or an alternate set for retesting.

Scores for Subtests: Individual/Group				
	Phonics		Vocabulary	
	Ind.	Group	Ind.	Group
100%	30	10	25	5
80%	24	8	20	4
60%	18	6	15	3

Level E—Unit 5

My Sidewalks offers two assessment options for each unit: a one-on-one Individual Test and a Group Test. Use just one of these options with your students. The Individual Test is the preferred option for use with intervention students since it will give you more precise information about their reading skills. You do not need to administer both tests.

Option 1 Individual Test

Directions This test is to be administered one-on-one to individual students. Make two copies of the test on page 70 and of the fluency passage on page 73, one for the student and one for you to mark. Read aloud the directions in **bold**.

- **This is a test about reading. In the first part, you will read a story aloud to me.**

Part One Fluency and Comprehension

Assess Fluency Take a one-minute sample of the student's oral reading of the passage on page 73.

- **I am going to ask you to read a story aloud to me.**
- **Use your best reading as you read this story titled "A Trip Back in Time."**

Have the student read aloud for one minute. Note miscues on your copy. After testing, record the words correct per minute (WCPM) on the Fluency Progress Chart on page 7.

Assess Comprehension Have the student read the selection quietly. If the student has difficulty with the passage, you may read it aloud.

- **Now I want you to read the story quietly to yourself.**
- **When you finish reading, I will ask you to tell me about what you read.**
- **Now read about the trip back in time.**

When the student has finished, or when you have finished reading it aloud, ask

- **Who was this story about? Tell me more about Dan.**
- **Where or when does the story take place?**
- **What is the problem or goal? How is the problem solved or the goal reached?**

Use the Narrative Retelling Rubric on page 8 to evaluate the student's retelling.

Part Two Phonics Words

Assess Phonics Skills Use the words at the top of page 70 to assess the student's ability to read words with this unit's phonics skills. Have each student read the words aloud. Mark errors on your copy. Record the student's score on the Word Reading Chart on page 78.

- **Now I'm going to ask you to read some words aloud to me.**
- **Point to the number one at the top of this page.**
- **Use your best reading to read the words in row 1.**

Continue in the same way for rows 2–5.

Part Three Phonics Sentences

Assess Phonics Skills Use the sentences in the middle of page 70 to assess the student's ability to read sentences with this unit's phonics skills. Have each student read the sentences aloud. Listen for the student's pronunciation of the phonics word in **bold** in each sentence. Mark errors on your copy. Record the student's score on the Word Reading Chart on page 78.

- **Now I'm going to ask you to read some sentences aloud to me.**
- **Point to the number six in the middle of this page.**
- **Use your best reading to read sentence 6.**

Continue in the same way for rows 7–10.

Part Four Concept Vocabulary

Assess Concept Vocabulary Use the words at the bottom of page 70 to assess the student's ability to read this unit's concept vocabulary. Have each student read the words aloud. Mark errors on your copy. Record the student's score on the Word Reading Chart on page 78.

- **Now I'm going to ask you to read some other words aloud to me.**
- **Point to the number eleven on this page.**
- **Use your best reading to read the words in row 11.**

Continue in the same way for rows 12–15.

Phonics Words

1. spoil   point   choice   royal   annoy

2. tension   fashion   nation   fraction   puncture

3. scoop   monsoon   screw   clue   continue

4. stalk   haunt   seesaw   taught   thought

5. neatness   commitment   ability   frailty   humorous

Phonics Sentences

6. Floyd saw the wind **destroy** his tree house.

7. In the **future**, Dawn will help me clean my room.

8. Andrew **outgrew** that small shirt last year.

9. I want to **launch** my new toy rocket.

10. Their noisy **argument** spoiled our dinner.

Concept Words

11. astonish   historical   reenactment   century   rendezvous

12. tracking   exploration   equipment   expedition   locate

13. companions   products   consumers   program   shuttle

14. chamber   stalactite   stalagmite   grotto   tunnel

15. enterprise   hardship   necessity   journey   route

Option 2 Group Test

Use this test if you prefer to assess in a group setting. Make copies of the test on pages 73–77 for each student. Since the Fluency and Comprehension test, which uses the passage on page 73, is to be administered individually, you will need two copies, one for the student to read and one for you to mark. Read aloud the directions in **bold**.

Part One Fluency and Comprehension

Assess Fluency Take a one-minute sample of the student's oral reading. This part of the test should be conducted with each student individually. Give the student a copy of the fluency passage "A Trip Back in Time" on page 73.

- **This is a test about reading.**
- **I am going to ask you to read a story aloud to me.**
- **Use your best reading as you read this story titled "A Trip Back in Time."**

Have the student read aloud for one minute. Note miscues on your copy. After testing, record the words correct per minute (WCPM) on the Fluency Progress Chart on page 7.

Assess Comprehension Have the student read the story quietly. If the student has difficulty with the passage, you may read it aloud.

- **Now I want you to read the story quietly to yourself.**
- **When you finish reading, you will answer some questions about what you read.**
- **Now read about the trip back in time.**

When the student has finished, or when you have finished reading it aloud, say

- **Now look at page 74.**
- **Answer questions 1–5.**

(Possible answers to questions 1–5 may be found on page 93.)

Part Two Phonics Words

Make sure students are on page 75.

- **Now we are going to do something different.**
- **I will read a number and a word aloud.**
- **I will say each word twice. Fill in the circle under the word I say.**

Pause after each item to allow students time to mark their answers.

1. **Fill in the circle under the word *joined . . . joined.***
2. **Fill in the circle under the word *fashion . . . fashion.***
3. **Fill in the circle under the word *too . . . too.***
4. **Fill in the circle under the word *thought . . . thought.***
5. **Fill in the circle under the word *sickness . . . sickness.***

Record the student's score on the Word Reading Chart on page 79.

© Pearson Education E

Part Three Phonics Sentences

Make sure the students are on page 76. Begin by saying

- **Now I will read a number and a sentence aloud.**

- **Follow along as I read each sentence. Then read the three words under the sentence.**

- **Find the word that best finishes the sentence.**

- **Fill in the circle next to the best word.**

- **Read the completed sentence aloud to me.**

Read the numbers and sentences below. Pause after each item to allow students time to mark their answers.

6. **Floyd saw the wind . . . *blank* . . . his tree house. Fill in the circle next to your answer. Now read the sentence back to me.**

7. **In the . . . *blank* . . . , Dawn will help me clean my room. Fill in the circle next to your answer. Now read the sentence back to me.**

8. **Andrew . . . *blank* . . . that small shirt last year. Fill in the circle next to your answer. Now read the sentence back to me.**

9. **I want to . . . *blank* . . . my new toy rocket. Fill in the circle next to your answer. Now read the sentence back to me.**

10. **Their noisy . . . *blank* . . . spoiled our dinner. Fill in the circle next to your answer. Now read the sentence back to me.**

Record the student's score on the Word Reading Chart on page 79.

Part Four Concept Vocabulary

Make sure the students are on page 77. Begin by saying

- **I will read a number and the definition of a word.**

- **Fill in the circle under the word that best matches the definition.**

Pause after each item to allow students time to mark their answers.

11. **Fill in the circle under the word that means a span of one hundred years.**

12. **Fill in the circle under the word that means a collection of tools, supplies, or other things needed for a certain purpose.**

13. **Fill in the circle under the word that means people who use goods or services.**

14. **Fill in the circle under the word that means a small cave.**

15. **Fill in the circle under the word that means difficulty or suffering.**

Record the student's score on the Word Reading Chart on page 79.

Name _____

A Trip Back in Time

Dan picked up his drum and joined the soldiers 9

in camp. This was his first Civil War reenactment, 18

and he was filled with excitement. His uniform and 27

equipment were new, but they looked old and 35

authentic. He was about to re-create a historic event 44

from another century. 47

Once in camp, Dan began to understand the 55

hardships people had faced during the Civil War. 63

The men slept in small tents or right on the ground. 74

There were no modern inventions like televisions in 82

sight. The soldiers relaxed by playing an early form 91

of baseball. Then Dan spotted different uniforms in 99

a camp at the other end of a grassy field. He felt a 112

sudden chill. Those soldiers were the "enemy." A 120

reenactment was enjoyable, but the real war had 128

been very serious. The captain gave an order, and 137

Dan took his place in front of the troops. He took a 149

step forward and marched back in time. 156

© Pearson Education E

Unit 5 Group Test

73

Comprehension

Directions Answer the following questions about the passage you just read.

1. What event did Dan take part in?

_____

_____

2. How was the reenactment like the Civil War? How was it different?

_____

_____

_____

3. What happened to make Dan move to the front of the troops?

_____

_____

4. What was Dan's role in the reenactment?

_____

_____

_____

5. How did Dan "step forward," yet march "back in time"?

_____

_____

_____

Phonics Words

1. joined   joyful   enjoyed
    ◯   ◯   ◯

2. fiction   fashion   fracture
    ◯   ◯   ◯

3. true   too   tool
    ◯   ◯   ◯

4. thawed   caught   thought
    ◯   ◯   ◯

5. sickness   segment   stillness
    ◯   ◯   ◯

Phonics Sentences

6. Floyd saw the wind _____ his tree house.

○ destroy

○ appoint

○ rejoice

7. In the _____, Dawn will help me clean my room.

○ fiction

○ nature

○ future

8. Andrew _____ that small shirt last year.

○ grew

○ new

○ outgrew

9. I want to _____ my new toy rocket.

○ lawman

○ laundry

○ launch

10. Their noisy _____ spoiled our dinner.

○ aridness

○ argument

○ amendment

Concept Words

11. historical   reenactment   century
         ○   ○   ○

12. exploration   equipment   expedition
         ○   ○   ○

13. companions   consumers   products
         ○   ○   ○

14. chamber   stalactite   grotto
         ○   ○   ○

15. hardship   enterprise   journey
         ○   ○   ○

Student's Name _____

Word Reading Chart for Unit 5 Assessment

Administer the Individual Test or the Group Test, not both.

Test Option 1 — Individual Test				
Phonics Words Circle the items the student missed.	**Total Items**	**Items Correct**	**Reteach**	**Retest**
1. Syllables with diphthongs *oi, oy* *spoil, point, choice, royal, annoy*	5			
2. Common syllables *-ion, -tion, -sion, -ture* *tension, fashion, nation, fraction, puncture*	5			
3. Syllables with *oo, ew, ue* in *moon, flew, blue* *scoop, monsoon, screw, clue, continue*	5			
4. Syllables with vowel sound in *ball: a, al, au, aw, ough* *stalk, haunt, seesaw, taught, thought*	5			
5. Suffixes *-ness, -ment, -ity, -ty, -ous* *neatness, commitment, ability, frailty, humorous*	5			
Phonics Words Total	**25**			
Phonics Sentences	**Total Items**	**Words Correct**	**Reteach**	**Retest**
6. Syllables with diphthong *oy* *destroy*	1			
7. Common syllables *-ture* *future*	1			
8. Syllables with *ew* in *flew* *outgrew*	1			
9. Syllables with vowel sound in *ball: au* *launch*	1			
10. Suffix *-ment* *argument*	1			
Phonics Sentences Total	**5**			
Concept Vocabulary	**Total Items**	**Words Correct**	**Reteach**	**Retest**
11. *astonish, historical, reenactment, century, rendezvous*	5			
12. *tracking, exploration, equipment, expedition, locate*	5			
13. *companions, products, consumers, program, shuttle*	5			
14. *chamber, stalactite, stalagmite, grotto, tunnel*	5			
15. *enterprise, hardship, necessity, journey, route*	5			
Concept Vocabulary Total	**25**			

Word Reading Chart for Unit 5 Assessment

Administer the Individual Test or the Group Test, not both.

Test Option 2 — Group Test				
Phonics Words Items 1–10. Circle the items the student missed.	**Total Items**	**Items Correct**	**Reteach**	**Retest**
Syllables with diphthongs *oi, oy* Items 1, 6	2			
Common syllables *-ion, -ture* Items 2, 7	2			
Syllables with *oo, ew* in *moon, flew* Items 3, 8	2			
Syllables with vowel sound in *ball: ough, au* Items 4, 9	2			
Suffixes *-ness, -ment* Items 5, 10	2			
Phonics Words Total	**10**			
Concept Vocabulary Items 11–15	**Total Items**	**Items Correct**	**Reteach**	**Retest**
century, equipment, consumers, grotto, hardship	5			
Concept Vocabulary Total	**5**			

- **RECORD SCORES** Use this chart to record scores.
- **RETEACH PHONICS SKILLS** If the student is unable to read words with particular phonics skills, then reteach the missed phonics skills.
- **PRACTICE CONCEPT VOCABULARY** If the student cannot read tested concept vocabulary, then provide additional practice.
- **RETEST** Use the same set of words or an alternate set for retesting.

Scores for Subtests: Individual/Group				
	Phonics		Vocabulary	
	Ind.	Group	Ind.	Group
100%	30	10	25	5
80%	24	8	20	4
60%	18	6	15	3

Level E—Unit 6

My Sidewalks offers two assessment options for each unit: a one-on-one Individual Test and a Group Test. Use just one of these options with your students. The Individual Test is the preferred option for use with intervention students since it will give you more precise information about their reading skills. You do not need to administer both tests.

Option 1 Individual Test

Directions This test is to be administered one-on-one to individual students. Make two copies of the test on page 82 and of the fluency passage on page 85, one for the student and one for you to mark. Read aloud the directions in **bold**.

- **This is a test about reading. In the first part, you will read a story aloud to me.**

Part One Fluency and Comprehension

Assess Fluency Take a one-minute sample of the student's oral reading of the passage on page 85.

- **I am going to ask you to read a story aloud to me.**

- **Use your best reading as you read this story titled "Trash or Treasure?"**

Have the student read aloud for one minute. Note miscues on your copy. After testing, record the words correct per minute (WCPM) on the Fluency Progress Chart on page 7.

Assess Comprehension Have the student read the story quietly. If the student has difficulty with the passage, you may read it aloud.

- **Now I want you to read the story quietly to yourself.**

- **When you finish reading, I will ask you to tell me about what you read.**

- **Now read about trash and treasure.**

When the student has finished, or when you have finished reading it aloud, ask

- **Who is this story about? Tell me more about Nick and Nicole.**

- **Where or when does the story take place?**

- **What is the problem or goal? How is the problem solved or the goal reached?**

Use the Narrative Retelling Rubric on page 8 to evaluate the student's retelling.

Part Two Phonics Words

Assess Phonics Skills Use the words at the top of page 82 to assess the student's ability to read words with this unit's phonics skills. Have each student read the words aloud. Mark errors on your copy. Record the student's score on the Word Reading Chart on page 90.

- **Now I'm going to ask you to read some words aloud to me.**

- **Point to the number one at the top of this page.**

- **Use your best reading to read the words in row 1.**

Continue in the same way for rows 2–5.

Part Three Phonics Sentences

Assess Phonics Skills Use the sentences in the middle of page 82 to assess the student's ability to read sentences with this unit's phonics skills. Have each student read the sentences aloud. Listen for the student's pronunciation of the phonics word in **bold** in each sentence. Mark errors on your copy. Record the student's score on the Word Reading Chart on page 90.

- **Now I'm going to ask you to read some sentences aloud to me.**
- **Point to the number six in the middle of this page.**
- **Use your best reading to read sentence 6.**

Continue in the same way for rows 7–10.

Part Four Concept Vocabulary

Assess Concept Vocabulary Use the words at the bottom of page 82 to assess the student's ability to read this unit's concept vocabulary. Have each student read the words aloud. Mark errors on your copy. Record the student's score on the Word Reading Chart on page 90.

- **Now I'm going to ask you to read some other words aloud to me.**
- **Point to the number eleven on this page.**
- **Use your best reading to read the words in row 11.**

Continue in the same way for rows 12–15.

Phonics Words

1. pregame   prejudge   midlife   midmorning   postscript

2. shook   overlook   football   push   bulldog

3. bind   wildly   boldness   untold   hosted

4. video   cruel   diary   meteor   graduated

5. local   locate   location   vision   visible

Phonics Sentences

6. My family eats a big **midday** meal on weekends.

7. Mom chose a bright new seat **cushion** for that chair.

8. Jeff tries not to say **unkind** things to anyone.

9. Janet just had a marvelous new **idea** for a story.

10. I visit the dentist when I have a **dental** problem.

Concept Words

11. encountered   misfortune   disappointed   solution   surprise

12. contaminate   thrive   promote   acre   wonder

13. valuable   currency   worth   monetary   exchange

14. conveyance   destinations   transcontinental   passengers   freight

15. advertisement   influential   commercials   gullible   persuade

Option 2 Group Test

Use this test if you prefer to assess in a group setting. Make copies of the test on pages 85–89 for each student. Since the Fluency and Comprehension test, which uses the passage on page 85, is to be administered individually, you will need two copies, one for the student to read and one for you to mark. Read aloud the directions in **bold**.

Part One Fluency and Comprehension

Assess Fluency Take a one-minute sample of the student's oral reading. This part of the test should be conducted with each student individually. Give the student a copy of the fluency passage "Trash or Treasure?" on page 85.

- **This is a test about reading.**
- **I am going to ask you to read a story aloud to me.**
- **Use your best reading as you read this story titled "Trash or Treasure?"**

Have the student read aloud for one minute. Note miscues on your copy. After testing, record the words correct per minute (WCPM) on the Fluency Progress Chart on page 7.

Assess Comprehension Have the student read the story quietly. If the student has difficulty with the passage, you may read it aloud.

- **Now I want you to read the story quietly to yourself.**
- **When you finish reading, you will answer some questions about what you read.**
- **Now read about trash and treasure.**

When the student has finished, or when you have finished reading it aloud, say

- **Now look at page 86.**
- **Answer questions 1–5.**

(Possible answers to questions 1–5 may be found on page 93.)

Part Two Phonics Words

Make sure students are on page 87.

- **Now we are going to do something different.**
- **I will read a number and a word aloud.**
- **I will say each word twice. Fill in the circle under the word I say.**

Pause after each item to allow students time to mark their answers.

1. **Fill in the circle under the word** *preheat . . . preheat.*
2. **Fill in the circle under the word** *hook . . . hook.*
3. **Fill in the circle under the word** *moldy . . . moldy.*
4. **Fill in the circle under the word** *trial . . . trial.*
5. **Fill in the circle under the word** *relative . . . relative.*

Record the student's score on the Word Reading Chart on page 91.

Part Three Phonics Sentences

Make sure the students are on page 88. Begin by saying

- **Now I will read a number and a sentence aloud.**

- **Follow along as I read each sentence. Then read the three words under the sentence.**

- **Find the word that best finishes the sentence.**

- **Fill in the circle next to the best word.**

- **Read the completed sentence aloud to me.**

Read the numbers and sentences below. Pause after each item to allow students time to mark their answers.

6. **My family eats a big . . . *blank* . . . meal on weekends. Fill in the circle next to your answer. Now read the sentence back to me.**

7. **Mom chose a bright new seat . . . *blank* . . . for that chair. Fill in the circle next to your answer. Now read the sentence back to me.**

8. **Jeff tries not to say . . . *blank* . . . things to anyone. Fill in the circle next to your answer. Now read the sentence back to me.**

9. **Janet just had a marvelous new . . . *blank* . . . for a story. Fill in the circle next to your answer. Now read the sentence back to me.**

10. **I visit the dentist when I have a . . . *blank* . . . problem. Fill in the circle next to your answer. Now read the sentence back to me.**

Record the student's score on the Word Reading Chart on page 91.

Part Four Concept Vocabulary

Make sure the students are on page 89. Begin by saying

- **I will read a number and the definition of a word.**

- **Fill in the circle under the word that best matches the definition.**

Pause after each item to allow students time to mark their answers.

11. **Fill in the circle under the word that means met unexpectedly.**

12. **Fill in the circle under the word that means to be successful or to flourish.**

13. **Fill in the circle under the word that means money or something that is used to buy goods or services.**

14. **Fill in the circle under the word that means the places a person is traveling to or the planned ends of a journey.**

15. **Fill in the circle under the word that means easily deceived or willing to believe anything.**

Record the student's score on the Word Reading Chart on page 91.

© Pearson Education E

Trash or Treasure?

On the first day of summer vacation, Mom   8

insisted that Nick and Nicole come to the flea market   18

with her. "It will be fun," she said. "You can start a   30

collection." The twins looked at each other and   38

frowned. They didn't know what a flea market was,   47

but they weren't gullible enough to think going to one   57

was a good idea.   61

When they got to the flea market, they saw that   71

it was like a huge yard sale. At first it all seemed like   84

junk, but when they looked more closely Nick found   93

a neat old toy and Nicole found a baseball card that   104

she hoped was valuable. They couldn't wait to see   113

what surprise they would find next. By the middle   122

of summer, both twins were serious collectors. They   130

even started to barter! The twins looked for a new flea   141

market advertisement every day. They had learned   148

that the old saying is true: One person's trash is   158

another person's treasure.   161

Name _____

Comprehension

Directions Answer the following questions about the passage you just read.

1. Why did Nick and Nicole first visit a flea market?

_____

_____

2. Why did they continue to visit flea markets?

_____

_____

3. What did they think when they first saw the items for sale? What did they think after they took a closer look?

_____

_____

_____

4. How might Nicole find out whether her baseball card is valuable?

_____

_____

_____

5. What does the expression "One person's trash is another person's treasure" mean?

_____

_____

_____

86

Group Test Unit 6

Phonics Words

1. postpone   preheat   present
    ○   ○   ○

2. hook   hound   hurt
    ○   ○   ○

3. boldly   moldy   mildly
    ○   ○   ○

4. triangle   trash   trial
    ○   ○   ○

5. relative   relation   related
    ○   ○   ○

Phonics Sentences

6. My family eats a big _____ meal on weekends.

○ midwinter

○ midterm

○ midday

7. Mom chose a bright new seat _____ for that chair.

○ pushing

○ cushion

○ ambush

8. Jeff tries not to say _____ things to anyone.

○ unkind

○ untied

○ unsold

9. Janet just had a marvelous new _____ for a story.

○ idea

○ area

○ annual

10. I visit the dentist when I have a _____ problem.

○ vision

○ dental

○ health

Concept Words

11.   encountered   misfortune   solution

          ○   ○   ○

12.   contaminate   thrive   promote

          ○   ○   ○

13.   currency   valuable   exchange

          ○   ○   ○

14.   conveyance   passengers   destinations

          ○   ○   ○

15.   advertisement   gullible   influential

          ○   ○   ○

Student's Name _____

Word Reading Chart for Unit 6 Assessment

Administer the Individual Test or the Group Test, not both.

Test Option 1 — Individual Test				
Phonics Words Circle the items the student missed.	**Total Items**	**Items Correct**	**Reteach**	**Retest**
1. Prefixes *pre-, mid-, post-* *pregame, prejudge, midlife, midmorning, postscript*	5			
2. Syllables with vowels *oo* in *foot*, *u* in *put* *shook, overlook, football, push, bulldog*	5			
3. Syllables with long *i: -ind, -ild;* Long *o: -ost, -old* *bind, wildly, boldness, untold, hosted*	5			
4. Syllables V/V *video, cruel, diary, meteor, graduated*	5			
5. Related words *local, locate, location, vision, visible*	5			
Phonics Words Total	**25**			
Phonics Sentences	**Total Items**	**Words Correct**	**Reteach**	**Retest**
6. Prefix *mid- midday*	1			
7. Syllables with vowel *u* in *put cushion*	1			
8. Syllables with long *i: -ind unkind*	1			
9. Syllables V/V *idea*	1			
10. Related words *dental*	1			
Phonics Sentences Total	**5**			
Concept Vocabulary	**Total Items**	**Words Correct**	**Reteach**	**Retest**
11. *encountered, misfortune, disappointed, solution, surprise*	5			
12. *contaminate, thrive, promote, acre, wonder*	5			
13. *valuable, currency, worth, monetary, exchange*	5			
14. *conveyance, destinations, transcontinental, passengers,* *freight*	5			
15. *advertisement, influential, commercials, gullible, persuade*	5			
Concept Vocabulary Total	**25**			

Student's Name _____

Word Reading Chart for Unit 6 Assessment

Administer the Individual Test or the Group Test, not both.

Test Option 2 — Group Test				
Phonics Words Items 1–10. Circle the items the student missed.	**Total Items**	**Items Correct**	**Reteach**	**Retest**
Prefixes *pre-, mid-* Items 1, 6	2			
Syllables with vowels *oo* in *foot*, *u* in *put* Items 2, 7	2			
Syllables with long *i*: *-ind*, Long *o*: *-old* Items 3, 8	2			
Syllables V/V Items 4, 9	2			
Related words Items 5, 10	2			
Phonics Words Total	**10**			
Concept Vocabulary Items 11–15	**Total Items**	**Items Correct**	**Reteach**	**Retest**
encountered, thrive, currency, destinations, gullible	5			
Concept Vocabulary Total	**5**			

- **RECORD SCORES** Use this chart to record scores.
- **RETEACH PHONICS SKILLS** If the student is unable to read words with particular phonics skills, then reteach the missed phonics skills.
- **PRACTICE CONCEPT VOCABULARY** If the student cannot read tested concept vocabulary, then provide additional practice.
- **RETEST** Use the same set of words or an alternate set for retesting.

Scores for Subtests: Individual/Group				
	Phonics		Vocabulary	
	Ind.	Group	Ind.	Group
100%	30	10	25	5
80%	24	8	20	4
60%	18	6	15	3

© Pearson Education E

Answer Key

Group Test Comprehension Questions

Unit 1, p. 26

1. The Iditarod is a dog-sled race across the Alaskan wilderness. [Main Idea]

2. It celebrates an event in 1925, when dog teams were used to bring medicine to the people of Nome. [Sequence]

3. Possible answer: Alike: Then, as now, people used dog sleds and traveled as quickly as possible across the same wilderness. They probably faced the same challenges as today's racers. Different: In 1925, the dog teams were racing to get medicine to people; today's racers do it for the challenge. [Compare and Contrast]

4. harsh blizzards, jagged mountains, frozen rivers, dense forests, and drifting snow

5. Possible answer: Everyone in the race gets the chance to do something exciting and challenging. [Draw Conclusions]

Unit 2, p. 38

1. They are people who help out after a disaster, such as a tornado, or another emergency strikes. [Main Idea]

2. Relief volunteers who live in the area hear about the emergency by telephone and head to the scene of the emergency whatever the time of day or night. [Sequence]

3. Possible answer: Alike: They probably go to regular jobs or go to school when they aren't volunteering. They care about others. Different: They have special training, so they know what they need to do to help out after a disaster. [Compare and Contrast]

4. They would probably bring food, blankets, bandages, and other basic things that people need to be safe and healthy. [Draw Conclusions]

5. At first they are frightened and in shock. After the volunteers arrive, many feel reassured that things are starting to improve. [Compare and Contrast]

Unit 3, p. 50

1. It is the most well-known painting in the world and may be the greatest painting. [Main Idea]

2. A worker at the Louvre Museum stole the painting. [Sequence]

3. It was probably much easier for the thief to carry and hide the picture without the frame. [Draw Conclusions]

4. Now it is displayed behind bulletproof glass, locked in a box. [Compare and Contrast]

5. People can see through it to view the *Mona Lisa*, but they can't get through it to steal or harm the *Mona Lisa*. [Draw Conclusions]

Unit 4, p. 62

1. He had an accident that left him with a physical disability. [Sequence]

2. Minnie was a monkey that was trained to help Mike with everyday tasks. [Main Idea]

3. She learned how to follow commands and do some things that people might need, such as turning on a computer and picking up things that had fallen.

4. Possible answer: Alike: Like a human assistant, Minnie could pick up things and do other things that Mike couldn't do for himself. Different: Minnie could understand some simple commands, but not as much as a person would. Mike used a laser pointer to help him communicate with her. [Compare and Contrast]

5. Possible answer: Yes. He giggled when he first met Minnie, and the author says the two became "lifelong friends." Mike probably thinks it's fun to have a monkey around. [Draw Conclusions]

Unit 5, p. 74

1. Dan took part in a Civil War reenactment. [Main Idea]

2. Possible answer: Alike: The camp and the people in it looked like they would have during the Civil War. Participants slept in tents or on the ground and didn't use modern inventions. Different: The "soldiers" were not really fighting a war. [Compare and Contrast]

3. The captain gave an order. [Sequence]

4. He was the drummer. [Draw Conclusions]

5. Possible answer: As he was stepping into the pretend battle, it really made him feel as if he were marching into the Civil War. [Draw Conclusions]

Unit 6, p. 86

1. They first visited because their mother insisted. [Sequence]

2. They continued because it was fun and they found interesting things. [Sequence]

3. Possible answer: First they thought that everything looked like junk. When they looked more closely, they found things that were interesting and possibly valuable. [Compare and Contrast]

4. She could try to sell it or barter with it at the flea markets she visits. [Draw Conclusions]

5. People see value in different things—one person might want to collect something that another person would throw away. [Main Idea]

Answer Key